Dennis to Alice

WRITTEN AND NARRATED BY
GEORGE S BOUGHTON

ILLUSTRATED BY MARTYN TILLIER
DESIGNED BY HOLLY TILLIER

Dedication

To the memory of this chance moment –
for reflecting on a better world

GBP NEWS

Peaceful River Wey

D

G

SCAN ME

This section of the River Wey, in the County of Surrey, United Kingdom, filmed late summer 2019, is where a series of events took place early in 2020.

A

Storms Ciara and Dennis - floods

This is just upstream of the River Wey as seen in the previous clip. It's now February 2020, storm Ciara caused some flooding, and this is a week later. Storm Dennis has just happened and we expect, at this point, for there to be severe flooding again.

This is the flooding on the same section of river two days after storm Dennis.

This is the flooding at dawn on the next day. The noise you can hear is a plane flying overhead.

A ▪▪▪▪▪▪▪▪▪▪▪▪

SCAN ME

SCAN ME

SCAN ME

Flood damage on the Wey

Early March:
This is two trees that came down after the floodwaters of storms Ciara and then Dennis.

SCAN ME

Fierce swan guards its territory

Mid March: Just one week after two trees came down across the river, a dam has already begun to form on the left there. And a swan seems to be guarding its territory from a goose; and we're imagining, judging by later events, that that's a goose that wants to lay a nest there. If it is, then that's the goose that we went on to call Alice.

R

SCAN ME

G

Felled trees obstruct boating

Mid March, and social distancing has begun to get people taking to the countryside to open spaces, as a release from isolation. This dam that's formed across the river has formed quite an obstacle course for them. Altogether though it has been an opportunity for people to get more connected with nature and it's good to see that.

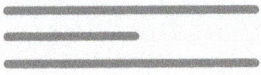

Dam exposes pollution levels

Just over a month has passed, now in April, and more material has come downriver adding to the dam.

There've been logs and timber, some cans… regrettably more plastic. That large trunk was there from the flood water but more has been added.

This is evidence of mankind's effect on the environment. The flooding can in part be attributed to climate change, which in part can be attributed to our impact on the atmosphere and on the ecology of the planet.

At least nature seems to be adjusting and this heron appears to be enjoying this addition to his territory. In the foreground there, there's a large trunk of a tree… and the stillness of the water on this side of the dam does seem to have attracted quite big fish. And I think that's what he's enjoying there.

I think we'll see a little later that there's been some beneficial effects of, for instance the COVID pandemic, on the environment. There're clearer skies but we'll come to that.

This is a moment of decision for the heron. Such patient creatures, often very statuesque.

That was it. But I don't think he got anything.

The Environment Agency was contacted in February, about the fallen trees and the dam it was creating, and they had said that they had been overloaded with work coping with the flooding. And then later in March they said that they were in isolation and unable to respond to this and other incidents but they would get round to it. As events unfold, it was rather opportune that they were that slow to respond, as we'll see in later clips.

SCAN ME

Alice and Arthur's nest

Shortly after the last clip these two geese seem to be taking a particular interest in this area. Two days later they seem to have adopted this island on the dam. And just two days later again, the female seems to have made herself at home. She seems to have made a nest, sat down on it and that's it. This is her home now, this is her nest. As time went on we named her Alice, mother goose Alice, and the male we decided is Arthur.

Keeping the world green, yet connected

Fifth of May and now, yes, we can see eggs there. Hard to count how many but she's now laid her eggs.

Alice is there comfortable. Arthur ever vigilant is on guard. There's also a female duck that seems to have made a nest next to Alice, which is interesting. Well the day has cleared, the skies are clear, and it's a beautiful scene. Verdantly green, Alice is on her nest, and reflected in the water are the blue skies we're beginning to see in the COVID pandemic.

Hardly any planes are flying; this is in the flight path for Heathrow airport and there are countless flights going overhead, everyday normally pre-COVID. But now, there's hardly a flight, any day; there're no contrails, no clouding up with the Sky. It's just incredibly blue and that's reflected in the water there. It's a joy, something we should try to insist on. It's important that flights resume at some point; we

SCAN ME

need to have the world connected.

We need to take this opportunity for the world to be more globally connected, to get peace in the world and equality in the world, enjoying each others cultures.

But without the contrails. Doing it in a green way.

A

16

Mega cities don't work

Seventh of May and it would seem that little duck, that had sat next to Alice, has now got her brood. There's Alice. Alice is comfortably on her nest, on yet another beautiful day. Just nearby is Arthur, on guard.

Alice and Arthur have been away from the nest. Every now and again they take a break. It's another beautifully blue sky. The wildlife probably doesn't appreciate these blue skies but we do; and we want to really revel in this magnificent wildlife and nature.

It's an opportunity that COVID has given everyone, to get out and enjoy the scenery but also the synergy of being with nature. We are from nature, we're part of nature.

We're now the custodians of nature; there's hardly anywhere on the planet that is so wild that it's not tended to by governments and people. But we mustn't misuse that. It's something we should rejoice in and make part of our daily lives.

Here're Alice and Arthur doing their daily wash, cleaning themselves. There's a train in the background. There's hardly any noise from planes anymore, they hardly fly. You hear the occasional train. It's also: The traffic on the M25 motorway is not far away and pre-COVID you could hear that traffic, it was part of what invaded the scenery – contrails in the sky, planes overhead roaring by, traffic on the M25. All of that's gone.

Now it's pure nature and it's beautiful. It's what we should have, it's what we've been with all through history. It's what this beautiful planet has miraculously put together, evolved. We must preserve it, we must treasure it.

She's just loving that. I believe that's Alice, with Arthur looking on. Sitting on the nest concentrating on her brood, on her eggs, and this is a moment of relaxing and getting away from that and getting herself clean. It's

a short respite. She has to go back to the nest but she's loving it. It's in her blood to look after them, and there it is.

More material has come down river, making the island even bigger. Not at that point, where the nest is, but to the right. And, it's evidence of how much is washed down the rivers. A lot of it is natural but there are timbers there and man-made materials that really shouldn't be there; but most particularly the plastics. It's extraordinary how long it's taking to get those out of our lives.

There she goes, Alice has decided she has to return. And that's a beautiful sight. That's her home, her castle; safe, away from the bank and predators. It's a special little spot; a fortunate happenstance that she could build a nest on a little island.

It's hard not to go back to it, seeing it every day, enjoying it every day, that blue of the sky reflected in the water. It's so… it's so… it's such a joy.

For centuries we have gravitated toward cities and the United Nation's projection is that in the next couple of decades 75% of the world's population will be living in cities, in mega cities. There are more mega cities under construction now than there have ever been. Civilizations through history have built cities and they've collapsed. They've collapsed because they've exhausted the resources needed to build them and to sustain them. But I think, more than that, they've collapsed because urban life doesn't actually work.

The country life, the little villages – where people are more connected, more involved in their communities, more involved in how they work and function, where they meet on the high street at the bakers or the butchers – that's what gives us the opportunity to be back close to nature, back in the country.

We should resume that, reverse the cycle of building and living in urban environments reliant on public transport, get back to individual mobility and the community.

SCAN ME

Rediscovering nature

Eighth of May: This is what we've been enjoying, while our household has been in isolation through the COVID pandemic, absolute peace and quiet and the beauty of nature untainted by noise, pollution, just itself. Alice there and Arthur, centre stage a joy to see.

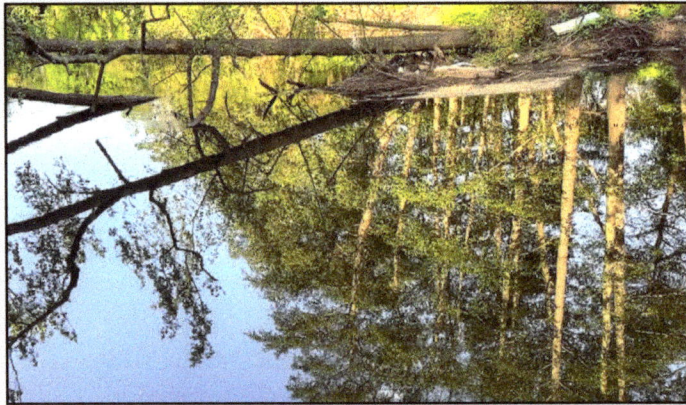

Ninth of May: Another day for Alice on her nest, checking on the eggs. Another day of peace for us, peace with nature.

In for a bath and something to eat. But where is Arthur?

Not unduly worried, everything's safe.

And still, where is Arthur? I think she's giving him a bit of flack. 'Where were you?'

Later the same day… That was more geese that had gone overhead, all calling to each other, and she wishes she could be with him; but this is more important.

I think that's Arthur just come back.

Time for her to go and join him.

There are dogs and people along the river here, not many, very few, all coexisting with nature; and that's what it needs to be, connected with nature. There's Arthur, coming up in the background.

Wey swan lake performance

Ninth of May: A swan, possibly the one suspected of chasing Alice away, is back for a special performance. Alice is not on her nest but the performance is there, possibly a rehearsal for her. This is where it starts…

SCAN ME

M

Spot all the wildlife

Twelfth of May: Alice is there on her nest, fast asleep.

Close by is a family of ducks; possibly the mother is the one that was nestled down next to Alice earlier on. It's certainly been a boon for creatures, this little island. There's been quite a variety visiting it.

It might be interesting to identify and see what creatures, what species, have been involved through the recording of these events.

And here's another creature.

Perhaps this squirrel is a little bit opportunist, looking for an easy meal.

SCAN ME

B

Fourteenth of May: What transpired here is that Arthur, maybe for reasons of protecting Alice and his brood, he came across behind the duck with her family, pushing them into the corner there – just caught it at the point where they got to the corner – and he seems to have evicted them.

SCAN ME

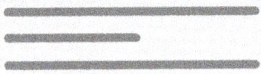

Geese under attack

Fox attack, Alice and Arthur retaliating

Arthur wards off a fox, Alice right behind him ready to join in.

Alice and her nest are under attack yet again. On the 18th, the same day, he's a persistent fox, or maybe not even the same fox. Arthur is there to protect them and the fox again shows no sign of wanting to give way. It's fortunate that they have this island, oasis fortress, to defend – easier to defend than on the land. But they're fully confident, they know what they're doing. There is no question that they're going to let this fox come any further. He seems persistent but… there he goes. Ferocious; there's no way he's going to let that Fox get anywhere near Alice and her nest. So, victorious again, again with his back to the enemy, fully confident, is the champ.

For the third time, Arthur wards off the fox and saves the day.

Goose families unite

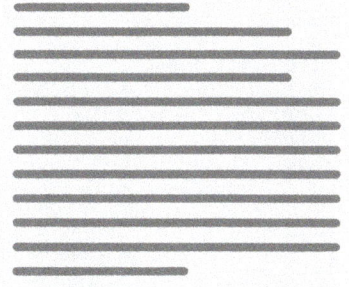

Twenty fifth of May: Alice is washing herself and to this side of her and, on the tree, is Arthur. There's the nest, perfectly fine. In the water there, there's a hint of blue sky. We'll see a little bit more of that in a moment.

Overhead can be heard the noise of a jet. There are very few going by and there're no contrails, just blue blue sky. And that's a buzzard flying up, overhead there. Wouldn't it be absolutely great if all the planes would fly without contrails, keep the skies blue

as they are?

That's the buzzard overhead again, majestic up there. There's a crow or blackbird or whatever; probably trying to ward him off, away from her nest. There's a pair of buzzards downstream there; and presumably they've got a nest there.

We came to realise that that family, there, are somehow connected with Alice and Arthur, and that seems to be Arthur calling out to them. They're distinctive in that one of the goslings appears to be quite a bit older than the others in that family.

SCAN ME

Alice's goslings

There they are. Alice's goslings, they've hatched. Roughly three weeks after she laid her eggs, they're there. Arthur, attentive as ever, on Guard.

No time to waste, it seems, Arthur's heading out. Maybe that's Alice's cue to move as well, she seems to be doing that.

And, yes, the little ones seem to be... yes, they're following. They've only just arrived in the nest and straight away they're getting the idea to leave it.

Apart from what might normally happen for new born goslings, where that pole is in the water, of recent days ripples in the water have shown that there's actually very little support under the nest. That the water is right under it and we've been concerned that, with more water coming down the stream and more debris, the nest could actually be weakening and could even collapse.

There they are. They've only just hatched and straight away there they are, at home on water.

Here is that other family, with the slightly older gosling. And here's Alice with her brood, having a little bit of a hard time getting back into her nest.

This is that whole joyful scene, finally at its climax, and this is the vantage point we've had.

SCAN ME

Alice and Arthur's farewell

This is that other family with the slightly older gosling. Strangely they seem to be visiting Alice's and Arthur's nest. And this is Arthur and Alice with their family. They'd left the nest shortly after the eggs had hatched, the same day in fact, on the 28th of May, and not been back until this time.

Arthur and Alice appear to be intent on getting to their nest…

There is very slow progress it seems.

Ah, the other family seems to be moving away. Allowing Alice and Arthur, with their family, to come through.

That was it. They'd been to their nest, seen it, and they're back on the water. And they never went back to the nest again.

And the other family left, as well, and they never came back… not to the nest.

SCAN ME

B

First published 2020

Published by GB Publishing Org

Copyright © 2020 George S Boughton

Written & Narrated by George S Boughton

Illustrations Martyn Tillier

Designed by Holly Tillier

Music 'Gliders' and 'In nature they trust' by Christopher Ritchie

ISBNs:

978-1-912031-49-8 (Hardback)

978-1-912031-48-1 (Paperback)

978-1-912031-21-4 (Video eBook)

978-1-912031-20-7 (Kindle)

GBP.

GB Publishing Org

www.gbpublishing.co.uk

www.ingramcontent.com/pod-product-compliance
Lightning Source LLC
Chambersburg PA
CBHW041637040426

42448CB00024B/3500